Silvia Via

The Proven Secret of an Outstanding

Linked in
Profile

How to Speed up your Social Media with AI

Disclaimer

All erudition contained in this book is given for informational and educational purposes only. The author is not in any way accountable for any results or outcomes that emanate from using this material. Constructive attempts have been made to provide information that is both accurate and effective, but the author is not bound for the inaccurate use/misuse of this information.

FOREWARD

First, I will like to thank you for taking the first step of trusting me and deciding to purchase/read this life-transforming eBook. Thanks for spending your time and resources on this material.

I can assure you the results, if you will diligently follow the blueprint. It has transformed lives, and I strongly believe it will equally transform your own life too.

All the information I presented in this eBook are for "Do It Yourself" and it is easy to digest and practice.

Prof. Silvia Vianello

Author Biography

Winner of the Top Middle East woman leader award and included in the prestigious list of Forbes among the 100 most successful Italian women in the world. PhD in economics, Dr Vianello is recognized worldwide as one of the leading experts in marketing, technology and future (especially on topics related to artificial intelligence, robots, blockchain, drones, machine learning, emotional intelligence). Often involved as a speaker to provide a new view on these topics. For example, she participated as a speaker at events organized by Intel, HP, Facebook, Google, Microsoft, Lenovo, Wurth, Top management forum, Tech data,

Salesforce, Nestle, NetCom e-commerce forum, Internet days, above Steria, Engineering Spa, Sisal, Oracle. She is currently Director of the Innovation Center at the prestigious Business School SP Jain School of Global Management, where she collaborates with top leaders of large companies to transform the corporate culture and create a better working world with new technologies. In her spare time, she is a 'Travel Influencer' and you can follow her on her Instagram account @profsilviavianello Previously, she was Managing Director of a Fortune 500 customer consulting firm. Also, she was Maserati Marketing Director for 24 countries in Asia, Middle East, Africa and Oceania. She has had many international experiences as a Professor and consultant in Paris, New York, Houston, Monaco, Zurich. She has conducted for many years a Tv Show on Sky "Smart & App, the technology show". She is also an author of many books and digital marketing articles published internationally. You can follow her also on:

LinkedIn profile:
www.linkedin.com/in/silviavianello/
Facebook profile:
www.facebook.com/vianello.silvia

Contents

CHAPTER ONE
What is LinkedIn?

With over 660+ millions registered members as of March 2020 (https://about.linkedin.com/), LinkedIn has been the most extensive professional community on the whole planet. However, there's more about LinkedIn than direct connections... After all, current advancements in media technology must provide more than size only.

LinkedIn can ease the exchange of ideas on a bigger scale. To put it differently, LinkedIn can also definitely boost professional and business opportunities for users.

The next question which should be answered is this: so, what? A high number of connections might appear remarkable, but how does this translate to real outcomes? LinkedIn is a valuable instrument to professionals since it provides the tools which might otherwise never have been obtained. The web site has characteristics which will permit you to get in contact with specialists that focus on the area that you are considering for your next career step. Unlike regular research, LinkedIn bogged the procedure through introductions and permits you to search for individuals by name, title, business, location, and other relevant information.

Among the effects of technology is that there's an extensive selection of information that's easily accessible. The drawback of this is that it might merely be a lot. You never know what sort of information will look about you if your title is searched. LinkedIn gives you command of all the info others may see about you. For people serious about the professional belief they wish to communicate, this is a priceless chance.

With a membership of over 660+ million as of March 2020, LinkedIn has become a valuable networking tool for everybody, and it's become vital for job hunters. There are too many folks on it to dismiss - and also many chances to associate together. Job seekers who know to take advantage of these changes - and learn how to create LinkedIn work for these - would be people who can experience the most success.

When most people think of social media, we consider for example mostly Facebook and Instagram. But while those are among the two of the most significant social networks, they're undoubtedly not the only ones in the market!

When it comes to business websites online, LinkedIn is most likely one of those best-known platforms in the market. It enables business professionals from each nation across the world, operating in each business, to attach with like-minded professionals, to share information, locate jobs and business opportunities, and advertise their businesses. It's also free to use, even though premium bundles are offering also excellent performance compared to the conventional free alternative.

Concerning operation, LinkedIn functions in a similar way to the majority of social media platforms. You join, create a profile, listing your employment history and accomplishments, and connect to your site, other social media accounts, and websites. The platform permits you to upgrade people you're linked to about projects you're working on, and it integrates with your current email account and joins you with connections that are already utilizing the platform.

Like other social media platforms, LinkedIn also lets users combine groups that are of interest to them; however, unlike Facebook, for example, each of the groups and classes on LinkedIn are professionally oriented. As an example, there are groups linked to an individual business or people-centered on particular geographic locations. These groups host talks, which can be of interest to their members, plus they enable group members to associate right with each other, together with business opportunities, employment offers, or even to talk about business-related problems and classes also give the ability to learn a new skill or software.

For the small business owner, being a part of LinkedIn has many added benefits as well.

First, it permits you to stay abreast of industry-related information and developments. If, for example, you work for the resort business, you can join groups that center on that business, and track, or get involved in, talks about the company industry and your own company as well. You might also participate with other resort business professionals, or even post your information, questions, or discussion topics.

You can take it a step further, but by linking groups and people linked to your business, in this circumstance, tourism growth teams, or courses for travel agents. You could then advertise your resort to professionals in these industries and open up new business avenues.

If you're looking for exceptionally trained and competent employees or salespeople that outsource solutions, then LinkedIn is also a beautiful place to locate them, and many business teams have committed boards for posting job opportunities.

For the person, LinkedIn provides the potential for locating employment, researching companies and industries they're considering, and linking with coworkers, and potential customers.

For the small business owner, it's a way of staying in touch with customers, providers, business news, and much more. It's a fantastic way to discover new business opportunities that you may otherwise have missed out on. Some groups are devoted to start-up companies, and to venture capitals, angel investments, and other kinds of the fund, so that there are additional benefits to people that want to start their little business also.

The trick to LinkedIn success begins with your profile. The more comprehensive, professional, and fascinating it is, the more probable it is going to impress prospective business partners of customers.

The following step, as soon as you have signed up and produced a profile, would be to make complete utilization of media features of LinkedIn. Join groups that are related to your business, and people that your customers will likely belong to. Connect your site and your site to your profile and become active on discussion boards.

Offering invaluable advice and donating to talks can help create your standing as an authority in your business, as well as any marketing pro will say, establishing your experience in any area is the first step to expanding your customer base.

LinkedIn, for example, like any other media, takes time, effort, and a bit of dedication. Members who invest a while regularly, creating new relations, leading to classes and talks, and maintaining their profiles present an intriguing will have much more success than people who register, and forget about it, rather than use the incredible support LinkedIn can offer!

To sum up, with so many possibilities in your palms, and also the chance to contact business people around the world from the comfort of the workplace, LinkedIn does provide individuals and company owners a valuable instrument, and it is worth learning the way the system functions and making it part of your total marketing program.

CHAPTER TWO
Benefits of using LinkedIn for your job search

If you are a business individual and you also are online, you've heard of LinkedIn. In reality, with 660+ million users around the world, the chances are excellent you've already established your LinkedIn account, here is a recap of the first chapter what is LinkedIn? As I said from the very first chapter, it's a network of people around the world willing to connect for professional purposes. While it is among the several social networking sites on the net, LinkedIn is most likely the best known and hottest business networking website.

So, another question, might reasonably be, "what's a business networking website?" and more precisely, "why should I care and how can it benefit me?" if you're asking these questions, then you're not alone! When there are enormous numbers of individuals creating LinkedIn accounts and constructing their networks, there are comparatively few that are receiving the best benefit from it. Because a lot of people still do not understand how to use it.

Following LinkedIn's explanation, the assignment of LinkedIn will be "to assist you to be effective in your everyday job and open doors to opportunities using the professional connections you currently have."

Even if you're not running a current job hunt, for continuing career management and private marketing efforts, any instrument which could help you network more effectively and economically should be of interest. In LinkedIn's words:

"When you combine, you create a profile that summarizes your professional achievements. Your profile makes it possible to find and be seen by former coworkers, customers, and partners. You can add more links by inviting trusted connections join LinkedIn and join you.

Your system includes your connections, your relations', and also the individuals they know, linking one to a large number of qualified professionals."

Through LinkedIn, subsequently, you can look for jobs, you may readily create personal "within" connections concerning job opportunities, you can promote your brand and credentials and be located and chased for project opportunities, and you're able to form relationships which are crucial to your career achievement and development.

But keep in mind, effective networking requires reciprocity through nurturing and developing win-win relationships. Through LinkedIn, you'll also have the chance to help those in your network, answering questions, supplying relevant prospects, and helping them make links to add whatever their objectives are.

From the definitive guide to utilizing LinkedIn for company and career management functions," I am on LinkedIn: now what?" I would say there are for example six significant advantages to using LinkedIn:

1) the capacity to be understood and improve your personal branding

2) the ability to be discovered by recruiters or other hiring governments or entities

3) the position to see others and make significant networking connections

4) the chance to learn new topics and share relevant industry insights

5) the ability to connect with group members

6) the opportunity to show you're plugged into the present technology and willing to help others in their goals as well.

If you already have LinkedIn accounts and also have a proven network set up, allow me to recommend you have a better look at how you're using it.

Especially the last point is extremely relevant. A community cannot be sustainable if all the members are there to take something out of it. And the truth is the majority of LinkedIn members are there only to take something out of it (searching for a new career opportunity, reading industry insights etc). We can say that members on LinkedIn follow the Pareto Principle: 80/20 rule. On LinkedIn, it means that 80% of the benefit comes from 20% of the people that you connect with. But it also means that 80% of the content is provided by 20% of the users. This is an incredible opportunity for all of us, since becoming an active LinkedIn member (eg. providing content, connection opportunities, etc) can boost a lot our visibility on this channel. Indeed, the LinkedIn algorithm is very generous with the 20% of users providing 80% of the content. We will explain this step further later in this book. For now, keep in mind the importance of giving to be successful on LinkedIn.

Are you there only to search for new job opportunities? Maybe you have improved your profile? Have you noticed any relevant groups? Participated in answering the questions and post of influencers? Or learning any new skills in the eLearning section of the website? LinkedIn is a great and quite useful networking application, but only if you utilize it!

In case you have an established LinkedIn accounts but have only let it sit unused, <u>now's</u> the time to log

on and find out ways to get the utmost advantage out of it. Now-before, you're actively job searching-is the very best time to focus on establishing and boosting your system. And, if you're new to LinkedIn and have not yet created an account, there's not any better time than the present! The more professionals who use LinkedIn, the more efficient it's going to be.

CHAPTER THREE
How to use LinkedIn to get hired

LinkedIn.com is among the fastest-growing recruiting tools now employed by headhunters and professionals alike. It's possible to enlarge your networks and your personal branding using LinkedIn. If you're still coming to grips with how to system or perhaps precisely what it is - then LinkedIn provides a fantastic foundation on which you can construct on your "offline" world. In the event you get informed at using LinkedIn as an expert improvement tool, then your chances are exponential.

Why use LinkedIn to get recruited?

Headhunters are now utilizing LinkedIn as one of the essential tools to supply a new gift for employers. Business owners and businesses also have become aware of exactly how useful LinkedIn would be to look for talented professionals to fill places - cutting out the middle person and significant marketing expenses. More than 130,000 recruiting agents, including agents from each fortune 500 business, are utilizing LinkedIn to supply their prospective contractors and employees.

Professionals, who have grown their own LinkedIn profiles and are operating in their relations, report on getting at least a contact weekly from headhunters or employers who've found them via LinkedIn. This is a superb tool to publicize your skills to a far bigger audience and provides opportunities for media yourself into your business of selection. As you get accustomed to LinkedIn, you will begin to understand this website potentials, along with your relations, can offer a personal introduction to the ideal individual at the perfect moment.

Have you heard of six degrees of separation? LinkedIn functions on the principle which by you inviting your contacts to connect you on LinkedIn, you also get access to their connections and so forth. Primarily, this builds up registration because of the lightning pace. Second, this produces a massive community of folks who can professionally help each other. LinkedIn is an expert-driven social networking website, so no movie uploads of late-night comments or household pics - only specialists linking into each other.

How do I begin using LinkedIn for professional advancement?

A simple membership on LinkedIn.com is free. You have to join and fill in your profile. If you are seriously interested in using LinkedIn for recruited, then take some opportunity to prepare your profile correctly, at the identical vain you'd offer your cv into some recruitment agent. The next step is to begin linking! LinkedIn works interactive programs that could upload your address book from several email programs such as outlook and the most common internet-based email programs. These tools automatically recognize some members of your address book, which are LinkedIn members. Proceed and carefully select who you wish to encourage to turn into a LinkedIn relationship. Notice: your connections will be visible to your contacts and they will have the opportunity to ask you to introduce them as well.

You can also ask another LinkedIn member to connect you with one of their contact, or reconnect with older colleagues, and colleagues using the colleague reconnect and classmate reconnect tools. In addition, you can search for the Alumni Page of the University you attended and get back in touch with your classmates. This is a superb way to enlarge your relations and you will never know who could be operating for what prospective employer. Profiles with more than 400 connections have an elevated likelihood of succeeding. Indeed, the average number of connections on LinkedIn is 400. There are plenty of opportunities to increase the number of connections on LinkedIn. Keep in mind the LinkedIn algorithm is more generous with active profiles with more connections and will boost your visibility.

Tip: do not merely enter someone's email address or business card in your contact manager - determine if they're also on LinkedIn. A couple of minutes per month can supply you with a massive network of links that may get into your profile and boost your personal branding.

Quite often I receive the question, should I accept a connection request from someone I personally do not know already "offline"? Well, my answer it pretty simple and straightforward. Do you usually check who is knocking at your door? You probably yes, and then if there is someone at the door and they offer you something you are not interested in, you can simply say "thanks, but no thanks" and you close the door. You can do the same on LinkedIn. You can open the door and accept the connection invitation and then if they bother you for any reasons (eg. Spamming or whatever) you can simply close the door. In other words, you can either disconnect with that person with the "remove connection" feature, or you can eventually also report or block that person. You can find these features if you click on the "More..." button, when you visit the profile of that contact also using the LinkedIn mobile app.

Keep in mind: the more connections you have, more visible you will be on LinkedIn, so start connecting!

How do I use LinkedIn to get recruited?

Listed below are some important advices on how to boost your odds to be recruited through LinkedIn. They apply to those who need professional improvement, consulting or sourcing professionals and business owners that wish to expand their reach:

1. Do not just sit in your profile - work your coworkers, former employers, clients, and professional contacts to get recommendations. Having recommendations in your own LinkedIn profile is golden concerning recruitment. You might even apply your LinkedIn profile as a central repository for guidance instead of needing to re-contact your referees every time you apply for work.

The company may also use this as a tool to centralize its reviews for potential candidates. You may then refer prospective employers or customers to a LinkedIn profile to see recommendations. Once again, being generous on LinkedIn is fundamental. So, if you want to be recommended, start recommending others first. Maybe past colleagues, or classmates, or whoever you fell deserve to be recommended by you. A lot of them will be glad to recommend you as well, boosting your profile.

2. Use keywords: when you're organizing your profile, make the most of LinkedIn search engine optimization where possible, while ensuring that your profile seems professional. By way of instance systems analyst familiar with business intelligence applications - operate at getting the attention of your intended audience. If you're in charge of a skilled or promotional website, you can link your site's URL for your LinkedIn profile. Again - key words - professional. You may even customize your LinkedIn profile by simply customizing the URL in the home page (right upper side of the screen) to reflect your title and make sure you allow your entire profile to be seen by general users.

3. If you're hunting for open positions on lots of the famous job sites, then the job insider toolbar on LinkedIn provides you an inside track. When you see a record, a job insider will look for your interior connections in the potential firm. Using your relations, you'll be able to gain information, and perhaps a helping recommendation to get an interview.

4. Combine applicable groups - you can join specialists, alumni, business, and company alumni groups recorded on LinkedIn. This is a superb way to display your profile and boost your connections. You could even make one- bringing together your very own significant network of liked minded professionals.

5. Folks have experienced incredible results from only merely asking and answering queries with other people posts on LinkedIn. Try for authenticity instead of self-promotion. And better a constructive feedback versus a negative comment.

6. Require the couple milliseconds to maintain an eye on the LinkedIn finds that come into your inbox. It is useful insider intellect to observe who is linking to whom and what your friends, colleagues, and former supervisors do. Pretty shortly with a large enough network, you may begin to construct your relations in the ideal direction.

7. Additionally, there are mega link boosting web sites like http://www.toplinked.com. Giving to help you enlarge your relationships exponentially so long as you agree to basic terms, like never decreasing an invitation to link to somebody referred by the website. Bear in mind the more links, the higher the chances for professional improvement and opportunities of being recruited.

8. Get to know that the "network statistics" beneath the individuals part of your LinkedIn profile. This will provide you with a review of the businesses your relations are linked to. By clicking in a company

of interest, you can watch the connections and the number of degrees of separation there are between them and you. Together with your shared connections as a foundation, it is possible to introduce yourself to relevant connections.

9. You can also choose to update your account to a premium at a price. This provides further features for recruiting on LinkedIn, depending on the type of premium account you select. If you are unsure if it is valuable and which type can be better, LinkedIn allows you to try them for free for a month.

10. The last term on profiles - it is not just about who you are working for or what you are presently doing. Every time you update your profile using a former employer or qualification, LinkedIn will automatically look for other men and women who worked there during precisely the same period. Your past history could start up the doorway to tomorrow's dream job! Again, keywords will also help the algorithm to match your capabilities with new job opportunities.

CHAPTER FOUR

Steps to create an outstanding LinkedIn profile

Everything on LinkedIn starts with the pattern. There are several components to making a good one; here is the way to get it done, in addition to some recommendations to bear in mind.

Begin with the fundamentals

After creating a profile, then be sure the email you provide on your profile is the one you frequently check; this is crucial to guarantee receipt of link requests, messages, and much more. Make sure you insert even more ways to show a potential employer how to get in contact, for example your website or any other channels you might be using it.

Primary demographic data, such as place, is self-explanatory why are so important to fill in.

Tip: if you are searching for a job, make sure there is a match between the location of your profile and the location of the position you are applying for. This will increase a lot the chance to get noticed, instead of being filtered out from the LinkedIn filters used by recruiters.

Additionally, as mentioned earlier, it is possible to start adding contacts in this early phase by enabling LinkedIn to get your email list. Make sure you do

that to reach quickly 500 connections. LinkedIn

prefers active members with a large community and if you have a massive network the algorithm will benefit your job search.

While filling out the demographic advice, LinkedIn will inquire about present employment status. Unemployed people might look at using phrases such as "now searching for job opportunities". Even though this reveals forward-thinking and optimism for the future, <u>unfortunately this statement will not support you in your job search</u>. Why? Because recruiters are searching for someone with specific skills and they will use those skill specific keywords to find the right candidate. For example, they might search for someone in the marketing field, and they will use marketing as a keyword to find a person with experience in marketing. If you have experience in marketing, it is then better to use for your headline for example "Marketing Specialist" or "Marketing Expert" even if you are currently unemployed.

Pick account type

This is where you need to make a selection between the first LinkedIn encounter, which can be free of  charge, or the premium alternative, which offers more features but costs a commission. Within the premium choice, there are numerous different alternatives to select from, such as sales professional, jobseeker, recruiters and much more. Each has a different price point and provides distinct advantages. Consider your planned use of LinkedIn when picking the account type that is ideal for the situation; recall that each supplies a free trial for one month, so that it is likely to cancel if it ends up that the very first choice was not the best one. Consider there is no need to upgrade to any premium version of the account to have an outstanding LinkedIn profile able to obtain incredible results.

Insert a photo

When it comes to photographs on LinkedIn, a professional is the title of this sport. Insert a professional headshot or one which appears that way. Do not get me wrong, sometimes a photo taken with a smartphone can utilize but there are some types of pictures it is better to avoid, such as selfies, or logo of the company, or pictures too dark, or too sexy (we have Instagram for that), or too far away, or with sunglasses at the beach. There's reason to check toward professional headshots first; individuals using a photograph taken by a professional get 14 times more perspectives than those using a ho-hum pic.

Use a photograph that's at least 200x200 pixels; anything less it'll look distorted and fuzzy. Recall those who add a high-quality picture to their profile capture 21 times more profile views as well as 36 times more messages than people who maintain the boilerplate look.

Another important point to consider is the file name when you upload your picture. To increase your chance to get noticed, you can rename your picture file with your name, last name, highest education level (eg. MBA), location where you would like to work, your top five skills. This will help you to give the right information to the algorithm regarding your profile. The same can be done also for the background picture, with the same type of keywords on the background picture file name to rank properly your profile in the LinkedIn search engine. Using an appropriate file name for both pictures will speed up your visibility and consequently your chance to get noticed by recruiters or potential clients.

Talk about expertise

For jobseekers, this is the place where the juice is – so be sure that the experience recorded reflects  whatever you can perform. It's possible to import a restart, or you could opt to bring each place. Many will start by introducing a reboot and then tweaking every site to include more information, optimize with keywords, and make it more readable compared to the standard empty; bare-bones could be. Always list the job experience beginning with the most recent. How to increase the chance to be visible by recruiters? Log in on LinkedIn and search for a job description of a job you would like to do. Check the requirements and skills requested for that specific position and see if they match or not with your current skills. If you have already that skill, please make sure you insert it on your LinkedIn profile, especially in the previous job experiences. If you do not have, there are many free online courses to fill in the gap (for example on https://www.skillshare.com/, or https://www.edx.org/, or https://www.udemy.com/ just to mention a few). If for example a job you would like to do require a software you are currently not able to use, you can go online and select the right course to fill-in the gap. Keep in mind once again: keywords load your current and past work history with terms you want to be found for. Use keywords when filling out your experience section and also your summary.

Time to get skills!

Take for a bare minimum of five abilities; the further recorded, the higher. You may now add up to 50 skills. People who have a minimum of five talents in their profile have been contacted 33 times more frequently by recruiters as well as other LinkedIn members, and get 17 times more profile views. Create a point of record skills in the sequence of competence and experience; these abilities are utilized to link jobseekers with recruiters as well as other relations, so it is essential to maintain the maximum highly honed abilities front and center. The top three can be flagged on your profile, make sure you select them wisely, aligned to the job you would like to do. Once again if you do not know which skills to select for your profile, search for the job description of similar jobs you would like to do and see what the required skills are. This way when you submit your application, those skills will immediately match, increasing your chances to get a new job.

If you are unsure about the skills you should insert on your LinkedIn profile, please take a look at the following pictures.

The Jobs Landscape in 2022

emerging roles, global change by 2022

Top 10 Emerging
1. Data Analysts and Scientists
2. AI and Machine Learning Specialists
3. General and Operations Managers
4. Software and Applications Developers and Analysts
5. Sales and Marketing Professionals
6. Big Data Specialists
7. Digital Transformation Specialists
8. New Technology Specialists
9. Organisational Development Specialists
10. Information Technology Services

declining roles, global change by 2022

Top 10 Declining
1. Data Entry Clerks
2. Accounting, Bookkeeping and Payroll Clerks
3. Administrative and Executive Secretaries
4. Assembly and Factory Workers
5. Client Information and Customer Service Workers
6. Business Services and Administration Managers
7. Accountants and Auditors
8. Material-Recording and Stock-Keeping Clerks
9. General and Operations Managers
10. Postal Service Clerks

As you can see in the above picture, the job landscape in 2022, according to the World Economic Forum, will look like this: a lot of technical capabilities will be required and those 10 types of jobs will be in very high demand. However, if you take a look at the below picture, the top 10 required skills in 2020 are related to soft skills, such as creativity, emotional intelligence, negotiation etc. Why? Because those are skills that cannot be replaced by any machine or robots, or artificial intelligence tool of any kind.

Top 10 skills

in 2020

1. Complex Problem Solving
2. Critical Thinking
3. Creativity
4. People Management
5. Coordinating with Others
6. Emotional Intelligence
7. Judgment and Decision Making
8. Service Orientation
9. Negotiation
10. Cognitive Flexibility

in 2015

1. Complex Problem Solving
2. Coordinating with Others
3. People Management
4. Critical Thinking
5. Negotiation
6. Quality Control
7. Service Orientation
8. Judgment and Decision Making
9. Active Listening
10. Creativity

Source: Future of Jobs Report, World Economic Forum

Recently also LinkedIn (reported the most important hard vs soft skills in very high demand for 2020 and are very similar to the ones reported by the World Economic Forum:

Source: https://business.linkedin.com/talent-solutions/blog/trends-and-research/2020/most-in-demand-hard-and-soft-skills

A nod to education

When such as education, make sure you include all colleges attended; this can allow for more natural connections together with older classmates, alumni classes, and so on. Additionally, include any instruction that was not necessarily via a college or university, like a corporate training seminar or a certificate earned through an institution or institution related to a field. You can also include certifications obtained online. For example, I added my License as a Certified Drone Pilot in the relevant section.

Licenses & Certifications   +

Drone-RPAS Remotely Piloted Aircraft System   ✏
Dubai Civil Aviation Authority
Issued Dec 2018 · No Expiration Date

Summarize it all

Listed below are a couple of points to remember while writing the best possible overview/summary for your profile to find the maximum focus:

❖ Do not be reluctant to demonstrate character! A whopping 40 percent of recuiters will enjoy a glimpse in your attitude.

- ❖ Be sure it's at least 100 words. This makes it increasingly likely to appear in searches.
- ❖ Dip a notice about specialties in the marketplace, as these keywords will appear in searches also. You can also include them as a bullet point at the end of your summary.
- ❖ Discuss expertise, but chat about your goals too.
- ❖ Include also in this section your email address to get in contact with you.

The headline topics

The headline is what's going to appear directly together with your name on LinkedIn, in addition to results on several search engines. It is a superb opportunity to create a fantastic first impression, so as far as possible, in just a few words. Make it snappy and intriguing, so relations wish to click on and discover out more. Weave in keywords, if at all possible. Listed below are a few examples:

❖ Marketing Specialist | Digital Marketing | Social Media Marketing Expert
❖ Civil engineering student, graduating 2020 | CAD, and blueprint specialist
❖ Talent Acquisition Manager in an award-winning startup

Insert additional, but relevant, info

LinkedIn provides the chance to put in many different pursuits to the profile, so do it! Those pursuits might catch the attention of a recruiter. Remember that hobbies can sometimes translate into skills which are exceptional in a working environment; for instance, a hobby of building model airplanes brings into an extreme focus on details, or an obsession with woodworking translates into taking the opportunity to have a job done the first time correctly. Make sure those hobbies can be somehow connected to your next career move, otherwise the LinkedIn algorithm may get confused on how to give visibility to your profile in their search engine.

Besides hobbies, also honors and awards are extremely powerful to boost your visibility and add credibility showing your achievements, so make sure you insert them, if any.

Make sure you will insert also the description of the awards or the competition. Here an example of how I inserted one of the awards I recently won:

Top 50 Women in Education at the World Education Congress
Jul 2019 • World Education Congress

The 50 Women in Education Leaders is an intensely researched process undertaken by the research cell which consists of Post Graduates in Management with over 5 years of experience posts their studies. It is the iconic job of the research cell to produce a shortlist of Individuals who are doing extraordinary work and track the record of their achievements. The shortlist is then reviewed by a Jury comprising of senior professionals from across the globe.

Criteria:
The criteria adopted in this case are:
· Strategic Perspective
· Future Orientation
· Track Record
· Integrity and Ethics
· Ability for Sustainable Education
· Evaluation Approach

Dr. Vianello won this award at the World Education Congress in 2019

For example, you can also add also scholarships obtained during your School Career, like this:

Four Year-Scholarship on the strength of Excellent and Outstanding Academic Records
1999 • Cà Foscari

Double-check, edit and assess again

Now the profile is nearly complete, return and double-check everything. Be sure that the dates of employment and schooling are right. Start looking for grammatical errors and typos – a glaring typo may draw attention away from this message. Use professional language. Double check your profile using another profile not connected with you, to see how your profile will look like when a recruiter is searching for a candidate like you.

Ultimately, possibly drop the summary and some other paragraphs across the profile to an internet checker, like Hemingway or even Grammarly, to examine whatever you may have missed or misspelled, if any.

Request someone to go through it again

One set of eyes is not enough. Ask friends already connected with you to have a look at the profile to be sure it's attractive and contains all pertinent info for your network. College students can speak to their career center to get help for this; professionals may turn to specialist services to be sure they're on the perfect path.

Produce a personalized URL

As mentioned earlier, a personalized URL makes it a lot easier for other people to find you. People that have a common name may discover their distinct URL is already recorded; nonetheless, including a place or numbers on the other side of the title may be a fantastic alternative. To try it, click on the "equipment" alongside the public profile then click on the penciled message near the URL. The personalized URL has to be between five and 30 characters, ideally with only your name and last name. If another person has the same name and last name and the URL is already taken, you can add for example your highest level of qualification

(eg. https://www.linkedin.com/silviavianellomba or https://www.linkedin.com/in/silviavianelloPHD)

Start building a network

Now it is time to begin making connections!

"LinkedIn is about specialist relations," said Kristan Wheaton, a professor at Mercyhurst University who teaches students about the best way best to use the support, "new users must connect to anybody they understand and anybody with whom they have a professional relationship. Including academics, recruiters, friends of the family, individuals in your business, essentially anyone."

Be active: gain insights from top industry leaders. There are so many out there, such as for example the one you can see here:

Update regularly

Utilizing LinkedIn regularly is recommended since this helps to keep you in the loop together with happenings and colleagues in the area. Post at least once per week or so, and take a look at messages, respond to requests for recommendations, create endorsements, comment on posts, send a congratulatory notice or update your profile when new items have been occurring.

"Status updates are an impactful way to share your expertise & stay top of mind on LinkedIn."

Purpose: to share concise, consistent updates with your network related to your interests or expertise.

Best practices for leveraging status updates:

- Post on a weekly basis.
- Be authentic. Establish your own voice, and write in the first-person.
- Focus on quality over quantity.
- Include an image within the post. Posts with imagery get significantly more traffic than posts that do not include imagery.
- Posts that include interesting / surprising facts, intriguing questions, and calls to action to read more tend to perform better.
- Write the post so that anyone reading it can understand it without prior context about a topic, campaign, etc.

What can you share via status updates? For example:

- Authored publications
- Industry insights
- Trending news

- Personal milestones
- Quotes or insights that inspire you
- Causes you care about

Article content

Finally, do not forget to begin publishing content. Maintain the material to items that are pertinent to a field, such as interesting articles, new figures or persuasive new inventions. Start a blog if you feel you can keep it up on a routine basis. Just be certain any material submitted is only as professional as possible.

You have three different options to become an active member on LinkedIn:

1. Share status update: share concise updates relevant to your expertise to generate engagement.
2. Interact with influencers and groups: follow influencers and join their post discussions to increase visibility and stay top of mind in a more focused environment based on your expertise and/or interests and geographical area.

3. Write a long form post: post short blogs content that reflect your expertise and interests.

How to create a perfect LinkedIn post?

A perfect LinkedIn post has the potential to reach a much wider audience and actually deliver your message in a much efficient way. Creating a perfect post is fairly simple and just need to follow some basic guidelines. Before writing the post, you must be sure of what audience you are targeting and what is the objective behind the post.

With that in mind, follow the 6 simple tips and tricks given below to capture the attention of the audience and deliver your message in the best possible way.

1. Always include a clear simple and effective call to action (CTA). When compared to a post without a call to action, including a CTA can drive double (2x) the engagement and a 55% higher rate of likes. Adding a link also drives your readers to be able to better connect with your objective and straight-away get engaged with your call for action. Every like and every comment will be free visibility for you on their network.

2. Starting a conversation by asking a question is also the best way to generate interest and engage the audience. So, ask thoughtful questions to involve your audience. Start by asking a question that is relevant to them and not just to you, where they can exchange their ideas and expertise. Again, every like and every comment will be free visibility for you on their network.

3. Attractive images make audience stop scrolling and actually read the content. If the objective is to deliver information, infographics work the best. As per research, pictures with people and faces receive more engagements and reactions. Stand out with an eye-catching image or some form of rich media (documents, presentations, articles, blogs...). It will help not getting lost in the feed. Images generally result in a 98% higher comment rate and 49% like rate. If the image is vertical it will occupy more space in their timeline, increasing your chance of being visible.

4. Post videos to encourage sharing. Links to videos playing directly on the LinkedIn feed

usually result in a 75% higher share rate and 32% higher like rate. People love videos and it's the best way to increase number of shares. Post relevant videos which shares your message and achieves the objective by capturing audience's interest and makes them engage with it. Make sure you embed the video directly on LinkedIn, instead of inserting a link driving people in a different website.

5. Make the post short, use bulleted or numbered points. LinkedIn bullet points are a great solution for posting the content. People will find it easier to confirm or not each of the mentioned points when they comment your post. More than that, make sure you use concise and very simple language, trim the content to only the most interesting and relevant parts for your audience, and avoid repetition. The level of attention on Social Media is decreasing, this suggestion will help you to get noticeable.

6. Lastly, be always active and post insightful comments on other posts. Engage with members through comments. This is a really

good way to start a conversation and make meaningful connections. Slowly but surely, your LinkedIn followers will increase, and you will have great connections with the relevant people from the given industry. Keep the conversation ongoing. Members expect brands to participate in conversations. Engage the audience to keep conversation going. Develop a plan for proactively handling any customer-service issues that may surface.

CHAPTER FIVE

How to optimize your LinkedIn profile

What do you do when you would like to find out more about a service or product? I bet that the first thing you do is go to Google (or another search engine) and look for it.

With so much information available to us now, search engines are an essential component of our life. If you search Google, you'll find info about literally anything in seconds.

Assessing your LinkedIn profile is comparable to optimizing your site or blog, which means that you can rank highly on Google (and of course on LinkedIn too).

Assessing your LinkedIn profile not only helps individuals locate your profile via the search feature, but it will also help LinkedIn urge folks to associate with, businesses you might be considering, or your ideal job.

Targeted recommendations

LinkedIn scans your profile also utilizes your keyword phrases, to make targeted recommendations for you. The more concentrated your profile is, the more focused the LinkedIn tips will be.

Once your LinkedIn profile is fine-tuned, you may observe targeted recommendations from your sidebar each time you log into. The LinkedIn algorithm is a powerful, artificial intelligence instrument.

Keyword choice

The most important part of search engine optimization is keyword choice. Search engines use keywords and phrases to locate and rank sites.

The crawler or spider-based hunt engines-so called since they sift through sites and add keywords to their databases-sort through millions of websites by following an algorithm or set of principles.

LinkedIn has its very own search algorithm, which positions user profiles on numerous variables, including your keywords. The more concentrated your keyword phrases are, the further your profile will probably stick out.

To improve your odds of getting your LinkedIn profile ranking highly, use your keywords in such segments of your profile:

- ❖ profile headline
- ❖ present work experience
- ❖ past work experience
- ❖ overview
- ❖ specialties
- ❖ file name of the pictures (profile picture and background)

Think about these questions while making your list of keyword phrases:

- ❖ Which are your abilities?

- ❖ What's your experience?
- ❖ What job titles best describe the situation you're searching for?
- ❖ Which makes you different from the competition?
- ❖ Which makes you better than the competition?
- ❖ What are your greatest accomplishments?
- ❖ In which city would you like to work?
- ❖ Does your next job require the ability to use a specific software?

If you think like most of the people out there today, you might face difficulty explaining your abilities and regions of experience, and that means you are fighting to produce your essential word list.

If you are struggling to develop a listing of everything you are excellent at, ask your friends or coworkers. They will be pleased to let you know precisely what you are good at (and everything you are not so great at if you are courageous enough to ask!).

LinkedIn ranking factors

Most of my students frequently ask me what decides the search positions on LinkedIn. A number of these ranking variables are as evident as I've shown in previous cases.

Utilize your target keywords as your last name area, on your specialist headline, and your profile outline.

As evident as these appear, LinkedIn does not formally tell us precisely what decides our search position.

LinkedIn utilizes proprietary algorithms to position and orders the results that you get when you seek out individuals on the website.

There is no single position for the LinkedIn search. Contrary to the standard search engines, we create significance scores distinctively for every member. Even though a question will yield the very same results for everyone, the arrangement is determined in part from the profile, action, and relations of the person searching. Testing a question from a couple of customers is unlikely to reflect the general rank any profile gets over the countless issues that LinkedIn has daily.

Searcher's significance is based on many different factors. Relevance is a proprietary algorithm that they are continuously improving. They intend to optimize search results for the searcher. Before it returns outcomes, they consider previous searcher's action on LinkedIn, the profiles returned from the question, along with other members that have run similar hunts in determining the sort order. These, together with other elements, combine to supply us with information to enhance the total quality of our associates' search results.

More keywords are not necessarily better. The risk is to create confusion in the algorithm. The advice is to include the keywords, including perennial keywords, on your profile, which best reflect your experience and experience. Should you incorporate an elongated collection of keywords into your profile, then you are probably showing up at a large number of searches. The question you want to ask yourself, however, is if members believe your profile pertinent for their search. Otherwise, their behavior as a collective group could be influencing the algorithm used to position one in search results.

Keep these items in mind as you boost your profile, and you are going to be found readily by the people you want to know.

Using AI Tools/Software to Generate Leads

What I find interesting is precisely how underestimated LinkedIn is. The popular Facebook, Instagram, Twitter, YouTube, TikTok captures all of the hype and attention, whether this golden mine softly stays and develops. My guess is the fact that as it's an expert media site, it generally does not have the universal sexual benefit of these others, however, also a savvy sales and marketing executive knows or ought to be aware of the energy of LinkedIn. Some of my students prefer to say: we do not like LinkedIn because LinkedIn is boring.

Because they do not know yet how powerful it could be if you know how to use it.

Generating more business would be everybody else's job at an organization irrespective of what your circumstance. Everybody else must not just be a new ambassador but, also, should be an outcome magnet. LinkedIn is currently primo for its B2b market as well as for B2c businesses. For vendors, tactical alliances, allies, investors, partners, employees, advisers and prospects, yes you can focus on LinkedIn.

LinkedIn has many plugins and features which are continuously changing and adapting to the growing needs of its user base.

But there is a range of tools that were created primarily to improve LinkedIn's built-in capabilities. Whether you intend to entice new prospects, generate new links on your business, or boost the effectiveness and ROI of your societal selling strategies, you might discover that using technical tools will improve your results and your overall experience in utilizing the LinkedIn platform.

Market study shows when you want to sky rocket your own profile to seem more engaging and get out into more audience there are internet site which may aid you with to generate leads, e-mail finding, send automatic link asks and send an automated message, and endorse the others in bulk, etc.

Here are some examples for this type of tasks.

1. Sales ql

The way Sales QL works is for you to download the extension on your google chrome browser, click on the extension icon and go to LinkedIn and pull up emails for any LinkedIn profile. Find personal and business emails and phones on LinkedIn will boost your recruitment and sales performance.

Here the link: https://salesql.com/

2. Octopus

Octopus is the all-in-one marketing software for LinkedIn, they have help thousands of LinkedIn users simplify prospecting efforts, grow their business with advanced marketing automation and lead generation tools.

Octopus is a powerful yet super simple autopilot for LinkedIn that automates your work and has a wide range of awesome features like sending automated (personalized) connection requests to second and third-level connections on LinkedIn, they also message hundreds of 1st level connections in bulk, automatically endorse up to 7 skills on profiles of your LinkedIn contacts and visit hundreds of profiles automatically. Here the link: https://octopuscrm.io/

3. eLinkPro

Another tool is eLinkPro, it helps your LinkedIn profile in the following ways: the first thing eLinkPro will do is to download your profile to excel, then using the principles of view backs in LinkedIn eLinkPro gets them to engaged with a link back to you to attract your audience and grows your connections, at the scale of social media. It downloads as a browser extension and profiles in LinkedIn are viewed by your browser as if you were viewing the profiles (over 5,000 per week). This starts a cycle. LinkedIn tells them you viewed their profile and the Prospects look back, become aware of you and start to view your profile, check out your profile and connect to you.

Here the link: https://elink-pro.com/

4. Dux-soup

Dux-Soup automatically views your LinkedIn prospect profiles, endorses their skills, follows their LinkedIn activity, and sends personalized messages on your behalf. It can also help you set up an automated LinkedIn drip campaign to your prospects that stops automatically when a candidate responds. Dux-Soup automate your LinkedIn lead generation leg-work, so you can focus on growing your business and closing deals. Dux-Soup is a google chrome extension you can easily download it here: https://www.dux-soup.com/

5. Linked dominator

The main aim of Linked Dominator to your LinkedIn profile is to expand your reach to your targeted audience to boost your sales, LinkedDominator can make you reach out to the million registered LinkedIn users. With over 660+ million members and 65% of them being key decision makers, it's been faster, more comfortable and more cost-effective to get your message in front of potential clients, journalists, partner's and even with future employees using LinkedDominator. LinkedDominator provides you the platform that allows you to create, execute and monitor different campaigns that are designed to automate various tasks on linkedin.

The benefits of using LinkedDominator are, increased profile/brand popularity, fast growing network of prospects, receive skill endorsements, free lead generation possibilities, and much more. It has helped thousands of small business and entrepreneurs to improve their LinkedIn marketing and publicity efforts so they can get more brand visibility, attract more targeted prospects, get more speaking engagements, instill credibility, increase client base, sales and of course and consequently generate higher profits.

Tools used by Recruiters

Recruiters use a variety of tools to access your application and profile. Most of these tools are driven by AI which gives a comprehensive analysis of the information shared by you in your profile. It is important to know about these tools in order to have a perfect LinkedIn profile visible to them.

Below are some examples of tools used by recruiters to attract applicants and shortlist profiles based on various aspects. The innovations in AI for recruiting are for example intelligent screening software that automates resume screening, but also recruiter chatbots that engage candidates in real-time, and digitized interviews that help assess a candidate's fit.

AI for screening for example automate screening reducing time to hire from 34 to 9 days only. Pre-assessment and screening plays a very critical role before making the final call. Crucial to set up your LinkedIn profile in order to be visible by those tools. In other words, do not expect there is a human there pre-filtering your profile. It is you against a machine. But using all the suggestions of this book, you will be able to be visible from those AI screening tools.

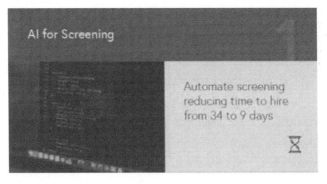

AI for Screening

Automate screening reducing time to hire from 34 to 9 days

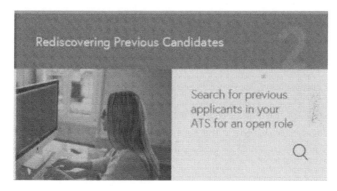

Automated tools can also support recruiters to search for previous applicants, rediscovering interesting profiles for an open role. In a nutshell, it's a form of pattern matching between a job's requirements and the qualifications of a candidate based on their resume. The goal of screening resumes is to decide whether to move that previous candidate forward, usually onto an interview or to reject them, assuming the candidate is still available. By matching with info on Social Media the machine will be able to guess if the candidate is still available or not.

Rediscovering Previous Candidates

Search for previous applicants in your ATS for an open role

Other tools commonly used by recruiters are recruitment chatbots. A recruitment chatbot, also called conversational agent is a software application designed to mimic human conversational abilities during the recruiting process. Similar to virtual personal assistants such as Alexa, Siri, and Google Now, a recruitment chatbot uses AI technology such as natural language processing to understand a user's request and know how to respond. It can mimic a human's conversational abilities; it's programmed to understand written and spoken language and respond correctly to request regarding for example an application for a job. Interest in chatbots is accelerating due to the benefits they hold for both recruiters and candidates. Candidates seem comfortable interacting with a chatbot since the #1 request from job seekers is more communication with recruiters. In a survey by Allegis, they found 58% of candidates were comfortable interacting with AI and recruitment chatbots for instance in the early stages of the application process. And 66% were comfortable with AI and chatbots taking care of interview scheduling and preparation.

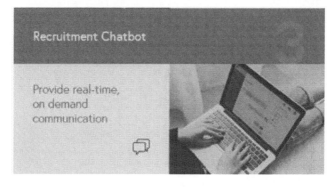

Applicants are aware the recruiting process might not be human-to-human at every touchpoint and value the opportunity to receive information in whatever way. Randstad found 82% of candidates believe the ideal recruiter interaction is a combination between innovative technology and a more personal, human interaction.

As that attitude continues to evolve, so will the recruitment chatbot.

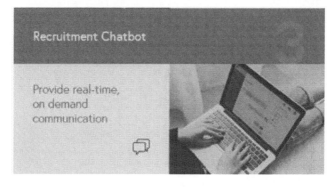

A software can also help recruiters with their administrative tasks such as collect information from candidates like their resume and contact information or ask questions about candidates' experience, knowledge, and skills and so. But it can also help ranking candidates on metrics such as qualifications, engagement, or recent activity or awards, answering questions about the job and the application process overall, scheduling an interview and so on. All of this can be collected in real life and simultaneously from hundreds to thousands of candidates. This information can then be sent directly to a human recruiter to follow up. Those software can also attract a more diverse talent pool by removing unconscious bias and increase diversity and inclusion in every organization.

De-Biasing Software

Attract a more diverse talent pool by removing unconscious bias

Over time, the machine learning component of those system will begin to understand which metrics it should be looking for based on the data it collects and rank candidates accordingly. This will also apply for super-targeting job advertising to re-target and geo-target candidates. Those adv will help recruiters to save a lot of time and money.

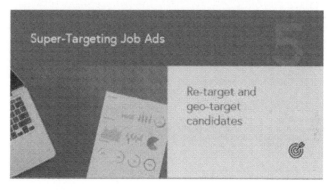

Industry estimates predict AI can automate up to 80% of top-of-funnel recruiting activities.

Consider also that the average cost of hiring can be more than $4,000 and the average time to hire more than 40 days. By automating a large part of qualifying and scheduling while simultaneously keeping candidates engaged, a software/chatbot/AI tool can dramatically lower both cost of hire and time to hire. It's important to keep in mind though that technologies are not designed to replace humans. No. But since it's estimated that 65% of resumes received for a role are ignored, by interacting with this ignored candidates, this marketing tool is doing the tasks that already time-strapped human recruiters don't have the time nor capacity to do in the first place.

Recruitment marketing software can more quickly screen out unqualified candidates, so recruiters can focus their efforts creating connections and building relationships with qualifies candidates to speed up the final process.

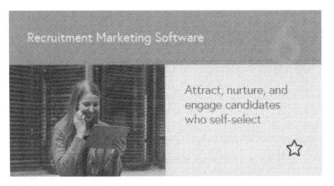

The major challenges of using AI in recruiting include the lack of standardization in texting, how "human" a chatbot is perceived, and not knowing how candidates will react to a machine instead of a human being. Because people have different ways of texting (slang, emojis, short form...), it's difficult to program a chatbot to understand each and every variation. Despite this, an increasing number of companies is already using those systems worldwide. As a candidate, you have to be ready to win your new job occupation, dealing also with machines, using the suggestions of this book to get visible and win against the algorithm filters.

Results are guaranteed if you use all the techniques and guidelines mentioned. Always stay active, be updated, and post relevant content to create meaningful connections.

With the help of the tools, you can easily make your profile much better than any other candidate. Make your profile stand out from all the others.

Below is the example of results from one of my students who used these guidelines.

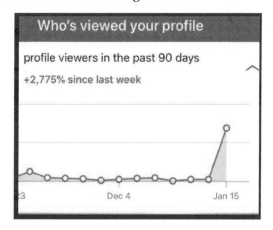

To check how your profile will improve using the suggestions proposed in this book, you can log in here with your LinkedIn account to check your social selling index: https://www.linkedin.com/sales/ssi

Your Social Selling Index (SSI) measures how effective you are at establishing your professional brand, finding the right people, engaging with insights, and building relationships. It is updated daily.

For example, you can have a result like this:

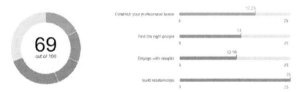

The tool will give you your score on your ability to establish your professional brand, find the right people, engage with insights, build relationships.

In addition, you can compare your score with people in your industry and people in your network.

People in your Industry

30
out of 100

Sales professionals in the
Management Consulting
industry have an average SSI
of 38.
You rank in the top 2%

⌄ Down 1% since last week

People in your Network

47
out of 100

People in your network have
an average SSI of 47.

You rank in the top 8%

⌄ Down 4% since last week

With the SSI tool you can improve your presence on
LinkedIn increasing your chance to get a job or better
leads for your company. But also discover when and
how to start a conversation with real-time insights.
And extend reach, building relationships that
accelerate sales by growing your network to reach
decision makers.

What is, at the end, the proven secret of an
outstanding LinkedIn profile? As mentioned since
the very beginning of the book, the best way to get
visible on LinkedIn is "Give. Give. Give". Be
generous on LinkedIn. Endorse friends for skills they
have, provide quality content, connect others to help
them on their goal. The more you give, the more you
get. Trust me. And you will be surprised by all the
amazing things that will happen in your life.

Drop me a line on LinkedIn with all your incredible
stories (add me using: vianello.silvia@gmail.com).

Printed in Great Britain
by Amazon